# The Ultimate Guide to Starting a Successful Online Business

**W**elcome to "The Ultimate Guide to Starting a Successful Online Business." In today's digital age, the opportunities for starting and running an online business are more abundant than ever before. The internet has opened up a world of possibilities, allowing entrepreneurs to reach a global audience and create thriving businesses from the comfort of their own homes. Whether you have a groundbreaking product idea, a unique service to offer, or a passion you want to turn into a profitable venture, this guide is here to help you navigate the exciting world of online entrepreneurship.

Starting an online business can be both exhilarating and challenging. It requires careful planning, strategic thinking, and a deep understanding of the digital landscape. In this guide, we will provide you with the essential knowledge, step-by-step guidance, and practical tips to set you on the path to success. Whether you're a seasoned entrepreneur looking to expand your business online or a first-time business owner, this guide is designed to equip you with the tools and insights you need to launch and grow a thriving online venture.

Throughout this guide, we will cover a wide range of topics, including finding your niche, conducting market research, creating a business plan, building your online presence, developing your product or service, setting up your e-commerce platform, crafting a marketing strategy, building customer relationships, managing finances, and embracing continuous learning and adaptation. Each chapter will provide you with actionable advice, real-life examples, and practical strategies to help you make informed decisions and navigate the unique challenges of the online business landscape.

Starting an online business is not without its obstacles, but with the right knowledge, mindset, and resources, you can overcome these challenges and build a successful and fulfilling business. Whether your goal is to achieve financial independence, create a lifestyle of freedom and flexibility, or make a positive impact on the world, the online business world offers endless possibilities.

So, if you're ready to embark on your online business journey, dive into this guide with an open mind and a willingness to learn. The digital landscape is ever-evolving, and the opportunities are ripe for the taking. Let's explore the world of online entrepreneurship together and set you on the path to creating a successful online business that aligns with your passions and goals.

# Chapter 1: Finding Your Niche

One of the crucial steps in starting a successful online business is finding your niche. Your niche is the specific area or market segment in which your business will operate. It's important to identify a niche that aligns with your interests, expertise, and the needs of your target audience. Finding the right niche will not only set you apart from your competitors but also increase your chances of success in the online business world. In this chapter, we will guide you through the process of discovering your niche and help you lay a strong foundation for your online business.

- Identify your passions and interests: Start by making a list of your passions and interests. What topics or industries excite you the most? Think about your hobbies, skills, and experiences. By choosing a niche that aligns with your passions, you'll have the motivation and enthusiasm to sustain your business in the long run.
- Conduct market research: Once you have identified a few potential niches, conduct thorough market research to assess their viability. Look for market trends, competition, and customer demands within each niche. Is there a demand for products or services in your chosen niche? Are there gaps or underserved areas that you can capitalize on?
- Define your target audience: Understanding your target audience is essential for online business success. Identify who your ideal customers are, their demographics, interests, and pain points. This will help you tailor your products, services, and marketing

strategies to meet their specific needs and preferences.

- Assess the competition: Research your competitors within your chosen niche. What are they offering? How do they differentiate themselves? Study their strengths and weaknesses to find opportunities for your own business. Differentiating yourself from the competition is crucial to stand out and attract customers.
- Consider profitability: While pursuing your passion is important, it's also essential to assess the profitability of your chosen niche. Will your business be able to generate sufficient revenue and profits? Consider the pricing dynamics, profit margins, and potential growth opportunities within your niche.
- Refine and narrow down your niche: Based on your research and analysis, refine and narrow down your niche to a specific target market. The more focused and specialized your niche, the better you can serve your customers and establish yourself as an expert in your field.
- Validate your niche: Validate your niche by testing it in the market. Consider conducting surveys, interviews, or launching a small pilot project to gather feedback and assess the market response. This will help you validate your business idea and make necessary adjustments before scaling up.

Remember, finding your niche is a dynamic process. It may require experimentation and adjustments along the way. Stay open to feedback and market trends, and be willing to pivot if needed. By finding the right niche, you'll set a solid foundation for your online business and position yourself for long-term success.

# Chapter 2: Conducting Market Research

Once you have identified your niche, it's time to dive deeper into market research. This chapter will guide you through the process of conducting comprehensive market research to gain insights into your target audience, understand industry trends, and assess the competitive landscape. Effective market research is crucial for making informed business decisions and positioning your online business for success.

- Define your research objectives: Clearly outline your research objectives to ensure you gather relevant and actionable data. What specific information do you need? Are you looking to understand customer preferences, market size, or competitor strategies? Defining your research objectives will guide your research process.
- Identify your target audience: Define your target audience in detail. Understand their demographics, behaviors, interests, and pain points. This information will help you tailor your products, services, and marketing efforts to meet their needs effectively.
- Analyze industry trends: Stay up to date with industry trends and developments. Follow industry publications, blogs, and forums to understand the latest innovations, challenges, and opportunities. This will help you stay ahead of the curve and adapt your business strategy accordingly.
- Use online surveys and questionnaires: Online surveys and questionnaires are effective tools for gathering data from your target audience. Create surveys using platforms like SurveyMonkey or Google Forms

and distribute them through social media, email newsletters, or your website. Ask relevant questions to gain insights into customer preferences, needs, and pain points.

- Conduct competitor analysis: Analyze your competitors to understand their strengths, weaknesses, and strategies. Study their products, pricing, marketing tactics, and customer feedback. This will help you identify gaps in the market and develop a unique value proposition.

- Utilize keyword research: Keyword research is crucial for understanding what your target audience is searching for online. Use keyword research tools like Google Keyword Planner or SEMrush to identify relevant keywords related to your niche. This will help you optimize your website content and drive organic traffic.

- Monitor social media and online communities: Keep an eye on social media platforms, online communities, and forums where your target audience interacts. Observe conversations, trends, and discussions related to your niche. This will provide valuable insights into customer preferences, needs, and pain points.

- Analyze data and draw conclusions: Once you have gathered the necessary data, analyze it to draw meaningful conclusions. Look for patterns, trends, and insights that can inform your business strategy. Use data visualization tools like Excel or Google Data Studio to present your findings effectively.

- Make data-driven decisions: Use the insights gained from your market research to make informed decisions about your product offerings, pricing, marketing channels, and customer engagement strategies. Data-driven decisions increase your chances of success and minimize risks.

- Continuously update your research: Market research is an ongoing process. Stay vigilant and continuously update your research as market conditions change, new trends emerge, and customer preferences evolve. Regularly reassess your target audience and industry landscape to stay ahead of the competition.

By conducting thorough market research, you gain valuable insights into your target audience and industry, enabling you to make informed business decisions. Remember, market research is not a one-time activity but an ongoing process that should inform your business strategy at every stage of your online business journey.

# Chapter 3: Creating a Business Plan

A solid business plan is essential for starting a successful online business. This chapter will guide you through the process of creating a comprehensive business plan that outlines your goals, strategies, financial projections, and more. A well-crafted business plan serves as a roadmap for your online business and helps you stay focused and organized as you navigate the entrepreneurial journey.

- Executive Summary: Start your business plan with an executive summary that provides an overview of your business concept, target market, unique value proposition, and financial goals. Keep it concise and compelling to grab the reader's attention.
- Company Description: Describe your online business in detail, including its mission, vision, and core values. Explain what makes your business unique and how it addresses the needs of your target audience.
- Market Analysis: Conduct a thorough market analysis to identify your target market, assess the competition, and understand industry trends. Provide insights into the size of your target market, customer demographics, and purchasing behavior.
- Products and Services: Outline the products or services you will offer in your online business. Describe their features, benefits, and how they meet the needs of your target audience. Highlight any unique selling points that differentiate your offerings from competitors.
- Marketing and Sales Strategies: Detail your marketing and sales strategies to reach and engage your target

audience. Identify the channels you will use to promote your business, such as social media, email marketing, content marketing, or paid advertising. Develop a pricing strategy and outline your sales approach.

- Operations and Management: Describe the operational aspects of your online business, including your organizational structure, team members' roles and responsibilities, and any external resources or partnerships. Explain how you will manage day-to-day operations and ensure smooth business processes.
- Financial Projections: Present financial projections for your online business, including revenue forecasts, expense estimates, and cash flow projections. Include details about your startup costs, pricing strategy, and sales projections. This section is crucial for attracting investors or securing financing.
- Risk Assessment and Mitigation: Identify potential risks and challenges that your online business may face. Develop strategies to mitigate these risks, such as contingency plans, insurance coverage, or diversifying your product offerings. This demonstrates your preparedness and commitment to long-term success.
- Implementation Plan: Create a detailed implementation plan that outlines the steps you will take to launch and grow your online business. Set specific milestones and timelines for key activities, such as website development, product launch, marketing campaigns, and customer acquisition.
- Monitoring and Evaluation: Establish metrics and key performance indicators (KPIs) to track the progress of your online business. Regularly monitor and evaluate your business's performance against these metrics and make adjustments as needed. This iterative process helps you stay agile and responsive to market changes.

Remember, a business plan is not set in stone but should evolve as your online business grows and adapts to market dynamics. Continuously revisit and refine your business plan to reflect new insights, goals, and opportunities. A well-designed business plan serves as a valuable tool for guiding your decisions and securing support from stakeholders, investors, or financial institutions.

# Chapter 4: Building Your Online Presence

In today's digital age, establishing a strong online presence is crucial for the success of your online business. This chapter will guide you through the process of building an effective online presence that attracts and engages your target audience. From creating a professional website to leveraging social media platforms, here are key strategies to help you establish a solid online presence:

- Design a Professional Website: Your website serves as the foundation of your online presence. Create a user-friendly and visually appealing website that reflects your brand identity. Ensure that it is mobile-responsive, optimized for search engines, and includes clear navigation, compelling content, and intuitive user experience.
- Develop Engaging Content: Content is king when it comes to building an online presence. Produce high-quality, valuable, and relevant content that resonates with your target audience. This can include blog posts, articles, videos, podcasts, infographics, or e-books. Consistently update your content to keep visitors coming back for more.
- Optimize for Search Engines: Implement search engine optimization (SEO) strategies to improve your website's visibility in search engine results. Conduct keyword research, optimize meta tags, use descriptive URLs, and create high-quality backlinks to improve your organic

search rankings. This helps potential customers find you when searching for relevant products or services.

- Leverage Social Media: Utilize social media platforms to expand your online presence and engage with your target audience. Identify the platforms where your audience is most active and create compelling profiles. Regularly share engaging content, interact with your followers, and use social media advertising to reach a wider audience.
- Build an Email List: Email marketing is a powerful tool for nurturing customer relationships and driving conversions. Offer valuable incentives, such as exclusive content or discounts, to encourage visitors to subscribe to your email list. Segment your list and send personalized, targeted emails to build trust and loyalty.
- Engage in Influencer Marketing: Collaborate with influencers or industry experts who have a strong online presence and a following relevant to your target audience. Partner with them for product reviews, sponsored content, or social media takeovers to increase your brand visibility and credibility.
- Implement Customer Relationship Management (CRM) Systems: Use CRM software to manage and track your interactions with customers and leads. This helps you deliver personalized experiences, track customer preferences, and nurture long-term relationships.
- Encourage Customer Reviews and Testimonials: Positive reviews and testimonials can significantly impact your online reputation. Encourage satisfied customers to leave reviews on platforms like Google, Yelp, or industry-specific review sites. Display testimonials on your website to build trust and credibility.
- Engage in Online Communities: Join online communities, forums, or social media groups relevant to your industry or niche. Contribute valuable insights, answer questions, and engage with community

members. This positions you as an expert in your field and increases your visibility.

- Monitor Online Reputation: Regularly monitor your online reputation by searching for mentions of your brand or business on search engines and social media platforms. Respond promptly and professionally to both positive and negative feedback to demonstrate your commitment to customer satisfaction.

Remember, building an online presence takes time and consistent effort. Continuously monitor your analytics, track your online performance, and adapt your strategies based on the data and feedback you receive. By establishing a strong and engaging online presence, you can effectively reach and connect with your target audience, ultimately driving the success of your online business.

# Chapter 5: Developing Your Product or Service

In order to create a successful online business, you need to develop a product or service that meets the needs and desires of your target market. This chapter will guide you through the process of developing a compelling offering that sets you apart from the competition. Here are key steps to consider when developing your product or service:

- Identify Your Target Market: Before you start developing your product or service, it's important to clearly define your target market. Conduct market research to understand their demographics, preferences, pain points, and buying behavior. This will help you tailor your offering to their specific needs.

- Define Your Value Proposition: Determine what makes your product or service unique and valuable to your target market. Identify the key benefits and advantages it offers compared to competitors. Clearly articulate your value proposition, highlighting how your offering solves a problem or fulfills a need.

- Conduct Competitive Analysis: Research your competitors to understand their strengths, weaknesses, and market positioning. Identify any gaps or opportunities that you can leverage to differentiate your offering. This will help you refine your product or service to stand out in the market.

- Develop a Minimum Viable Product (MVP): Instead of waiting to perfect your offering, start by developing a minimum viable product (MVP). An MVP is a scaled-down version of your product or service that allows you to test its viability and gather feedback from early adopters. This helps you iterate and improve based on real-world user insights.

- Focus on User Experience: User experience plays a crucial role in the success of your online business. Design your product or service with a user-centric approach, ensuring it is intuitive, easy to use, and provides a seamless experience. Consider user feedback and iterate on your offering to continuously enhance the user experience.

- Price Your Offering Strategically: Determine the pricing strategy that aligns with your target market and positions your product or service competitively. Consider factors such as production costs, perceived value, market demand, and your business goals. Regularly review and adjust your pricing strategy based on market trends and customer feedback.

- Test and Refine: Once you have developed your product or service, conduct thorough testing and gather feedback from a select group of users or customers. Use this feedback to identify areas for improvement and make necessary refinements. Iterate on your offering to ensure it meets the evolving needs and expectations of your target market.

- Develop a Scalable Business Model: As you develop your product or service, consider the scalability of your business model. Explore ways to streamline operations, automate processes, and leverage technology to support growth. This will enable you to scale your online business as demand increases.

- Consider Intellectual Property Protection: Depending on the nature of your product or service, it may be beneficial to consider intellectual property protection, such as patents, trademarks, or copyrights. Consult with a legal professional to determine the best approach to protect your unique offering.

- Continuously Innovate: The digital landscape is constantly evolving, and customer preferences can change rapidly. Stay abreast of market trends, industry developments, and customer feedback. Continuously innovate and adapt your product or service to stay ahead of the competition and meet the evolving needs of your target market.

By following these steps and dedicating time and effort to developing a compelling product or service, you can position your online business for success. Remember to stay customer-focused, seek feedback, and iterate based on market demands. With a well-developed offering, you'll be one step closer to building a thriving online business.

# Chapter 6: Setting Up Your E-commerce Platform

Once you have developed your product or service, it's time to set up your e-commerce platform. This chapter will guide you through the essential steps to establish a robust and user-friendly online store. Here are key considerations when setting up your e-commerce platform:

- Choose the Right E-commerce Platform: Select an e-commerce platform that aligns with your business needs and goals. Consider factors such as ease of use, scalability, customization options, payment gateways, security features, and customer support. Popular e-commerce platforms include Shopify, WooCommerce, BigCommerce, and Magento.
- Design a Professional and User-Friendly Website: Create an appealing and user-friendly website design that reflects your brand identity. Ensure that your website is visually appealing, easy to navigate, and optimized for mobile devices. Pay attention to the user experience, including fast page loading times, intuitive navigation menus, and clear calls-to-action.
- Streamline the Purchase Process: Make it easy for customers to make a purchase on your website. Simplify the checkout process by minimizing the number of steps required, offering guest checkout options, and providing secure payment gateways. Implement a reliable inventory management system to track product availability and prevent overselling.

- Optimize for Search Engines (SEO): Implement search engine optimization (SEO) strategies to improve your website's visibility in search engine results. Research relevant keywords, optimize your product descriptions and titles, and generate high-quality content to attract organic traffic. Consider integrating SEO plugins or tools to assist with optimization.
- Secure Your Website: Protect your website and customer data by implementing robust security measures. Install SSL certificates to encrypt data transmission, use secure payment gateways, and regularly update your website's software and plugins. Implement strong passwords and enable two-factor authentication to enhance security.
- Enable Analytics and Tracking: Set up analytics tools such as Google Analytics to track visitor behavior, conversions, and sales. Analyze data regularly to gain insights into your customers' preferences, identify areas for improvement, and make data-driven decisions to optimize your online business.
- Integrate Social Media and Marketing Tools: Leverage the power of social media by integrating social sharing buttons and social media widgets on your website. Develop a strong social media presence and create engaging content to attract and engage your target audience. Utilize email marketing tools to build a subscriber list and communicate with your customers effectively.
- Offer Multiple Payment Options: Provide a variety of payment options to accommodate your customers' preferences. Accept major credit cards, digital wallets, and alternative payment methods such as PayPal or Apple Pay. Ensure that the payment process is secure, reliable, and user-friendly.
- Implement Customer Support Channels: Set up customer support channels to address inquiries, concerns, and provide assistance. Offer options such

as live chat, email support, and a dedicated customer support phone line. Promptly respond to customer inquiries and provide exceptional customer service to build trust and loyalty.

- Test and Optimize: Regularly test your e-commerce platform to identify any usability issues, bugs, or performance bottlenecks. Conduct A/B testing to optimize elements such as website layout, product pages, and call-to-action buttons. Monitor key metrics and user feedback to continually refine and improve your e-commerce platform.

Setting up an effective e-commerce platform is crucial for the success of your online business. By selecting the right platform, designing a user-friendly website, securing customer data, and providing excellent customer support, you'll create a positive online shopping experience for your customers. Continuously monitor and optimize your e-commerce platform to stay competitive and drive sales.

# Chapter 7: Creating a Marketing Strategy

Now that your online business is up and running, it's time to create a marketing strategy to promote your products or services and attract customers. In this chapter, we'll explore key elements to consider when developing your marketing strategy. Here are essential steps to create an effective marketing plan:

- Define Your Target Audience: Identify your target audience based on demographics, interests, and buying behaviors. Understand their needs, pain points, and preferences to tailor your marketing messages effectively.
- Set Clear Marketing Goals: Determine specific, measurable, achievable, relevant, and time-bound (SMART) goals for your marketing efforts. Whether it's increasing brand awareness, driving website traffic, or generating sales, clearly define your objectives.
- Conduct Market Research: Gain insights into your industry, competitors, and target audience through market research. Analyze market trends, competitor strategies, and customer behavior to identify opportunities and differentiate your business.
- Develop a Strong Brand Identity: Create a compelling brand identity that resonates with your target audience. Define your brand values, mission, and unique selling proposition (USP). Consistently communicate your brand message through your website, social media, and other marketing channels.

- Choose the Right Marketing Channels: Select the most effective marketing channels to reach your target audience. Consider a mix of digital marketing channels such as social media, search engine marketing (SEM), content marketing, email marketing, and influencer partnerships.
- Create Engaging Content: Develop high-quality, relevant content that provides value to your target audience. Craft blog posts, videos, infographics, and other content formats that address their needs, answer their questions, and demonstrate your expertise.
- Implement Search Engine Optimization (SEO): Optimize your website and content for search engines to improve your organic visibility. Conduct keyword research, optimize your meta tags, headings, and URLs, and build high-quality backlinks to improve your search engine rankings.
- Leverage Social Media Marketing: Establish a strong presence on relevant social media platforms to engage with your target audience. Create and share compelling content, run targeted ads, and foster genuine connections with your followers.
- Utilize Email Marketing: Build an email subscriber list and leverage email marketing campaigns to nurture relationships with your customers. Send personalized emails, share exclusive offers, and provide valuable content to keep your audience engaged.
- Monitor and Measure Results: Regularly track and analyze the performance of your marketing efforts. Use analytics tools to measure website traffic, conversion rates, social media engagement, and other relevant metrics. Adjust your strategies based on data insights to optimize your marketing campaigns.
- Adapt to Emerging Trends: Stay updated with the latest digital marketing trends and technologies. Embrace new platforms, features, and strategies to stay ahead

of the competition and reach your target audience effectively.

- Customer Relationship Management (CRM): Implement a CRM system to manage customer interactions, track sales leads, and enhance customer retention. Use CRM data to personalize marketing messages and improve customer satisfaction.

Remember, a successful marketing strategy requires ongoing evaluation, experimentation, and adaptation. Continuously monitor your marketing campaigns, gather customer feedback, and refine your strategies to ensure long-term success.

By following these steps and developing a comprehensive marketing plan, you'll effectively promote your online business, attract customers, and drive sustainable growth.

# Chapter 8: Building Customer Relationships

Building strong and meaningful relationships with your customers is crucial for the long-term success of your online business. In this chapter, we'll explore strategies to foster customer loyalty, provide excellent customer service, and cultivate a positive reputation. Here are essential steps to build and maintain customer relationships:

- Provide Exceptional Customer Service: Make customer satisfaction a top priority. Respond promptly to inquiries, address concerns or issues, and go the extra mile to exceed customer expectations. Offer multiple support channels, such as email, live chat, or phone, and ensure your customer service team is knowledgeable and friendly.
- Personalize the Customer Experience: Tailor your interactions and offerings to meet individual customer needs. Use customer data and insights to personalize marketing messages, recommend relevant products or services, and show genuine interest in their preferences and feedback.
- Create a Loyalty Program: Implement a loyalty program to reward and incentivize repeat purchases. Offer exclusive discounts, early access to new products, or loyalty points that can be redeemed for future purchases. Encourage customers to refer your business to their friends and family.
- Gather Customer Feedback: Regularly solicit feedback

from your customers to understand their experiences and gather insights for improvement. Use surveys, feedback forms, or social media polls to collect feedback. Act on their suggestions and demonstrate that their opinions matter to your business.

- Engage on Social Media: Use social media platforms to connect and engage with your customers. Respond to comments, messages, and reviews in a timely and professional manner. Share user-generated content, run contests, and create a sense of community around your brand.

- Offer Exclusive Content and Resources: Provide valuable content and resources that are exclusive to your customers. This could include educational materials, tutorials, guides, or access to a members-only area on your website. Show your customers that you are invested in their success and well-being.

- Implement a Customer Relationship Management (CRM) System: Use a CRM system to effectively manage customer interactions and track their purchase history, preferences, and interactions with your business. Leverage this data to personalize your marketing efforts and offer tailored recommendations.

- Show Appreciation: Express gratitude to your customers for their support. Send personalized thank-you emails, offer surprise gifts or discounts, or acknowledge loyal customers publicly on your website or social media platforms. Make your customers feel valued and appreciated.

- Continuously Improve: Actively seek ways to improve your products, services, and customer experience based on feedback and market trends. Stay updated with industry developments, listen to customer suggestions, and proactively address any issues or gaps in your offerings.

- Monitor and Respond to Online Reviews: Regularly

monitor and respond to online reviews, both positive and negative. Address any negative feedback promptly and professionally, and publicly acknowledge and thank customers for their positive reviews. Use reviews as an opportunity to learn and improve.

Building strong customer relationships requires ongoing effort and dedication. By prioritizing exceptional customer service, personalization, and engagement, you can cultivate loyal customers who will not only continue to support your business but also become advocates and refer others to your brand.

Remember, building customer relationships is a continuous process. Regularly assess and refine your strategies based on customer feedback and evolving market trends. By investing in strong customer relationships, you'll create a loyal customer base that will contribute to the growth and success of your online business.

# Chapter 9: Managing Finances and Scaling Your Business

Managing your finances effectively is crucial for the long-term success and growth of your online business. In this chapter, we'll explore key financial considerations and strategies to help you navigate the financial aspects of your business and scale it to new heights. Here are essential steps to manage finances and scale your online business:

- Create a Financial Plan: Develop a comprehensive financial plan that outlines your business's financial goals, revenue projections, expenses, and cash flow projections. Set realistic targets and regularly review and update your plan as your business evolves.
- Track and Monitor Expenses: Keep a close eye on your business expenses. Maintain accurate records of all expenses, including operational costs, marketing expenses, inventory costs, and any other relevant expenditures. Use accounting software or tools to track and categorize expenses effectively.
- Monitor Cash Flow: Cash flow management is vital for the financial health of your business. Regularly monitor your cash inflows and outflows to ensure you have enough funds to cover expenses and invest in growth opportunities. Implement strategies to optimize cash flow, such as offering incentives for early payments or negotiating favorable payment terms with suppliers.
- Maintain Accurate Bookkeeping: Keep your financial records organized and up-to-date. Implement proper

bookkeeping practices, including recording all sales, purchases, and transactions accurately. Consider hiring an accountant or using accounting software to ensure accuracy and compliance with tax regulations.

- Explore Funding Options: As your business grows, you may need additional capital to fund expansion or invest in new opportunities. Explore different funding options, such as loans, grants, crowdfunding, or seeking investors. Evaluate the pros and cons of each option and choose the one that aligns with your business goals and financial situation.

- Invest in Technology and Infrastructure: As your business scales, invest in the right technology and infrastructure to support your growth. This may include upgrading your website, improving server capacity, implementing efficient inventory management systems, or investing in automation tools to streamline operations.

- Diversify Revenue Streams: Consider diversifying your revenue streams to reduce reliance on a single product or service. Explore opportunities to introduce complementary products or services, develop partnerships, or expand into new markets. Diversification can help mitigate risks and create new growth avenues for your business.

- Monitor Key Performance Indicators (KPIs): Identify and track key performance indicators that are relevant to your business. This may include metrics such as customer acquisition cost, customer lifetime value, conversion rates, average order value, or website traffic. Regularly assess these KPIs to gain insights into your business's performance and make data-driven decisions.

- Develop a Growth Strategy: Create a clear growth strategy that outlines your objectives, target markets, marketing tactics, and expansion plans. Identify opportunities for scaling your business, such as entering new markets, launching new products or services, or expanding your customer base. Regularly review and adjust your growth strategy as needed.

- Seek Professional Advice: Consider seeking professional advice from financial advisors, accountants, or business consultants who specialize in online businesses. They can provide valuable insights, guidance, and expertise to help you navigate financial challenges, manage growth, and make informed financial decisions.

Remember, managing finances is an ongoing process. Regularly review your financial performance, analyze trends, and adjust your strategies accordingly. By effectively managing your finances and scaling your business, you can position yourself for long-term success and achieve your business goals.

# Chapter 10: Embracing Continuous Learning and Adaptation

In the fast-paced world of online business, staying ahead of the curve requires a mindset of continuous learning and adaptation. Embracing new knowledge, skills, and trends can help you maintain a competitive edge, innovate, and navigate the evolving landscape. In this chapter, we'll explore strategies to foster a culture of continuous learning and adaptability in your online business. Here are key steps to embrace continuous learning and adaptation:

- Cultivate a Growth Mindset: Adopt a growth mindset, which is the belief that abilities and skills can be developed through dedication and hard work. Embrace challenges, view failures as learning opportunities, and maintain a positive attitude towards personal and professional growth.
- Stay Informed: Keep yourself informed about industry trends, market changes, and emerging technologies. Follow industry publications, blogs, podcasts, and attend webinars or conferences related to your field. Actively seek new information and insights to stay up-to-date with the latest developments.
- Invest in Professional Development: Allocate time and resources for ongoing professional development. Take courses, workshops, or certifications that enhance your knowledge and skills in areas relevant to your business. This could include digital marketing, e-commerce, data analysis, or any other domain that aligns with your

business needs.

- Network and Collaborate: Engage with peers, industry experts, and fellow entrepreneurs to exchange ideas, share experiences, and learn from each other. Join online communities, participate in forums or social media groups, and attend networking events to expand your professional network and gain valuable insights.
- Experiment and Test: Be willing to experiment with new strategies, technologies, or business models. Test different approaches and measure their effectiveness. Embrace a mindset of experimentation, learn from the outcomes, and iterate based on the results to optimize your business processes.
- Seek Feedback: Regularly seek feedback from customers, clients, and partners. Their insights can provide valuable perspectives on your products, services, and overall business performance. Actively listen to feedback, identify areas for improvement, and make necessary adjustments to meet customer needs and preferences.
- Foster a Learning Culture: Create a culture of learning within your organization or team. Encourage employees to pursue professional development opportunities, provide access to training resources, and establish regular knowledge-sharing sessions. Encourage open communication and collaboration to foster a learning-oriented environment.
- Monitor Competitors: Keep an eye on your competitors and industry leaders to learn from their successes and failures. Analyze their strategies, products, and customer engagement techniques. This can provide valuable insights and inspiration for your own business.
- Embrace Change and Adaptation: Be open to change and willing to adapt your strategies based on market dynamics, customer feedback, and industry trends. Recognize that the business landscape is constantly

evolving, and your ability to adapt quickly can be a significant competitive advantage.

- Reflect and Evaluate: Regularly reflect on your business performance, achievements, and areas for improvement. Conduct periodic evaluations to assess the effectiveness of your strategies and identify opportunities for growth and innovation. Use data-driven insights to inform your decision-making process.

By embracing continuous learning and adaptation, you can foster innovation, remain agile, and position your online business for long-term success. Remember, learning is a lifelong journey, and staying curious and adaptable will enable you to thrive in the dynamic digital age.

Congratulations! You have reached the end of "The Ultimate Guide to Starting a Successful Online Business." Throughout this guide, we have explored the essential steps and considerations for launching and growing an online business. From finding your niche and conducting market research to building your online presence, creating a business plan, and managing finances, you now have a solid foundation to embark on your entrepreneurial journey.

Starting an online business is an exciting endeavor that offers countless opportunities for growth and success. However, it also requires dedication, perseverance, and continuous learning. Remember that success doesn't happen overnight, and building a thriving online business takes time and effort.

As you move forward, keep in mind the following key takeaways:

- Find your passion and niche: Identify a market gap and align your business with your passions and strengths.
- Conduct thorough market research: Understand your target audience, competitors, and industry trends to make informed decisions.
- Create a comprehensive business plan: Outline your goals, strategies, and financial projections to guide your business operations.
- Build a strong online presence: Invest in professional website design, optimize for search engines, and leverage social media and digital marketing to attract and engage your audience.
- Develop high-quality products or services: Focus on

delivering value and meeting customer needs to build a loyal customer base.

- Prioritize customer relationships: Nurture your customer relationships through excellent customer service, personalized experiences, and feedback-driven improvements.
- Continuously adapt and innovate: Stay informed about industry trends, embrace new technologies, and be open to change to stay ahead in the dynamic digital landscape.
- Manage your finances effectively: Keep track of your finances, monitor cash flow, and seek professional advice when needed to ensure the financial health of your business.
- Embrace continuous learning: Stay curious, seek knowledge, and invest in your personal and professional development to sharpen your skills and stay competitive.
- Believe in yourself: Have confidence in your abilities and believe in the potential of your business. Stay resilient, motivated, and adaptable in the face of challenges.

Remember that building a successful online business is a journey filled with learning opportunities and growth. Stay committed to your vision, be persistent in your efforts, and be open to adapting your strategies along the way. Surround yourself with a supportive network and seek guidance from mentors or experts when needed.

With passion, perseverance, and a well-executed plan, you have the potential to create a thriving online business and achieve your entrepreneurial dreams. Best of luck on your journey, and may your online business flourish and bring you fulfillment and success!